Growing up in
ANCIENT ROME

Brenda Ralph Lewis

B. T. Batsford Ltd *London*

ISBN 0 7134 3374 4

Printed and bound in Great Britain by
Anchor Brendon Ltd,
Tiptree, Essex
for the Publishers Batsford Academic and
Educational, an imprint of
B T Batsford Ltd,
4 Fitzhardinge Street, London W1H 0AH

Frontispiece **Roman boy, 1st century AD**

Acknowledgment

The Author and Publishers thank the following
for their kind permission to reproduce copyright
illustrations: BBC Hulton Picture Library for figs 2,
5, 6, 8, 11, 14, 15, 24, 25, 29, 31, 32, 33, 36, 43,
45, 46, 59, 60; Pat Hodgson Library for figs 12, 21,
57; A.F. Kersting for fig 3; The Mansell Collection
for figs 4, 7, 10, 13, 16, 17, 18, 19, 20, 27, 28, 30,
34, 35, 39, 40, 47, 48, 49, 51, 52, 54, 55, 58. The
other pictures illustrations appearing in the book are
from the Publishers' collection. Thanks are also
expressed to Pat Hodgson for the picture research
on the book.

Contents

The Illustrations

1 Rome, the Centre of an Empire

Ancient Rome, the heart of the great Roman Empire was never quiet, calm or asleep for a single moment.

All night hundreds of wheeled vehicles rumbled through the narrow streets. By sunrise the last of them were only just leaving the city. Wheeled traffic was forbidden in Rome between sunrise and four o'clock in the afternoon. Therefore it was during the hours of darkness that the million and more people who lived in Rome in the mid-second century AD received their daily deliveries of wine, food, meat and other necessities. But they probably got very little rest.

If the Romans were not disturbed by the noise of the traffic and the shouts of the drivers, they were perhaps kept awake by the last customers reeling away from a night's merry-making at their local drinking dens.

And if they escaped that disturbance, they would be disturbed, not long afterwards, by the hullaballoo of the day's first visitors arriving in the city.

For at sunrise the traffic in Rome was two-way traffic. The vehicles rumbled out and the visitors flooded in. Long before the sun came up, the roads leading into Rome were packed with herds of cattle, pedestrians, horsemen and litters borne by slaves. Meanwhile, inside Rome, the city's beggars prepared to receive the day's visitors. They stirred themselves in the doorways and corners where they had spent the night and wandered towards the outskirts of Rome. There, they positioned themselves at the side

1 A carriage approaching a milestone (see picture 58)

of the approach roads, all keeping a keen eye out for the wealthiest visitors. Among them sat beggar children, many of them sent by their parents to wheedle money or food out of some farmer or, better still, a Roman noble, senator or governor from a distant province of the Empire. Some of these children, like the adults, pretended to be blind, deaf or crippled. Some were genuinely handicapped, for the monotonous diet of porridge eaten by the poor in Rome was thought to cause blindness and malformations.

Nearer the centre of Rome more fortunate children prepared to go to school. They scrambled from bed, threw on their tunics and wriggled their feet into their sandals. Then they washed their hands and faces in bowls of water and headed towards the "triclinium" (dining-room) to have their breakfast. The household slaves had already set the dining table with plates of bread and pancakes and dishes full of honey and dates. One slave stood by with a jar of wine which had been mixed with water.

After breakfast the older boys put on their togas. These were large, semi-circular woollen blankets, which were wrapped around the body. Boys wore togas with a purple stripe along the edge until they were sixteen years old. After that, their togas would be plain white.

When they were ready, the children picked up the wax tablets on which they wrote and made sure that they had not forgotten their stilus, the metal stick they used for writing in the wax, and their "abacus" or counting frame. Forgetting anything they needed during lessons could mean a caning from the teacher or some other punishment.

This was only one way in which schoolchildren could get into their teacher's bad books. Discipline in Roman schools was very

2 Rome in the reign of the Emperor Septimus Severus (AD 146-211). People entered the city through the arches in the city wall at the end of all the approach roads

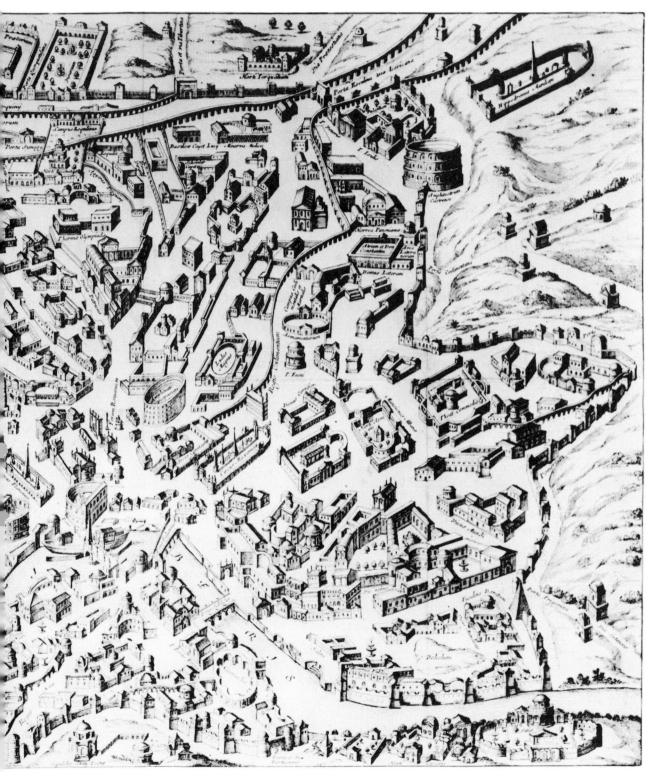

7

◄ 3 The Arch of Titus, one of the entrances into Rome. It was built in the 1st century AD, to commemorate the conquest of Palestine

severe. Teachers had no patience with lazy or forgetful students or those who larked about during lessons. At the slightest sign of trouble or restlessness, the cane appeared, or the equally painful bundle of birch twigs which teachers also used to beat their pupils.

School started at dawn, and the pupils arrived in the forum to find that the teacher had already set up his school in one corner. There were wooden stools for the pupils to sit on, and a sort of windbreak to separate the school from the people passing by. The windbreak was a cloth stretched out onto a wooden frame.

Learning reading, writing and mathematics in these conditions was like studying in the middle of a busy main road. Pupils who studied in the small rooms at the side of the forum were a little better off. But the only children who could learn lessons in proper peace and quiet were the ones whose teachers came to their home every day. Everyone else had to work with an enormous amount of noise going on around them.

4 A toga was draped round the body and back ► across one shoulder

5 A pupil is beaten
▼

The fora were the central places in Rome. Here, merchants and businessmen met to discuss their transactions. Orators came to make speeches about politics or some other important matter. Poets declaimed their newest verses to enthusiastic audiences. Afterwards the poets might be seen standing by one of the Greek slaves who wrote down the poems as their authors dictated them. Market traders set up their stalls and kept up an endless shouting to advertise their wares. There were yells of anger and pain as barbers who had set up their chairs in the forum cut a customer's face with their blunt knives.

All the time people went to and fro across the forum, making for the basilica (law courts), the temples, the libraries and the many other public buildings surrounding it.

There were always crowds of tourists gazing at Rome's magnificent statues, fountains, arches, monuments and other buildings. The tourists could also watch buildings being constructed and see the great pulleys with which the labourers lifted heavy stones. At the bottom of the pulley there was a wheel with men inside "walking" it round and round. The tourists had plenty of shops to look at too: caulkers, furriers, chandlers, stonemasons, locksmiths, blacksmiths, silversmiths and innumerable others.

6 The central forum in Rome (the Forum Romanum — see picture 2)

7 Part of a tomb, showing builders using a pulley. ▶ The men inside the wheel are walking it round

Customers crowded in and out of the shops. There was the noise of cobblers hammering at their lasts as they made sandals and boots. There was the din of people in the wine shops fighting and arguing because they had had too much to drink. In the streets outside people gambled or played dice, and more quarrelling and fighting went on over some disputed decision.

From the bakeries and cookshops came the clunking and grinding of the large stone mills and, particularly distracting for schoolchildren, the delicious smells of hot, freshly made cakes and bread.

There were other, less pleasant smells — from the dirty water gushing along the drains down one side of the streets, and beneath the road from the sewers which flowed towards the river Tiber. The people who seemed to be hurrying along every street in the city were not always sweet-smelling either. Not everyone bathed regularly, and some people never bathed at all.

Once every nine days there was a market day and no school. Many of the visitors to the markets of Rome came to buy new slaves to labour on their country farms or work as servants in their villas. Some came to buy teachers for their children, some to buy scribes to deal with their correspondence

8 Big millstones at the bakery in Pompeii

and organize their business affairs. These teachers and scribes were often Greeks, who were the best educated people in the vast Roman Empire.

In the slave market in Rome it was possible to see how extensive and varied the Roman Empire was. Apart from the Greeks, there were Celts from Britain, dark-skinned Iberians from Spain and blonde, brawny Germans. There were swarthy Numidians and Egyptians from the Roman territories in North Africa, and there were Parthians, Bithnyans, and Phoenicians from Turkey and Palestine.

The slaves stood on platforms in the slave market, with cards round their necks giving their personal details: their age, their nationality, their temperament and any special skills they might possess. Buyers came to inspect them. They poked their muscles to see if they were strong, looked at their teeth to see if they were healthy, and wondered if they could get them for less than the price written on their cards.

The buyers most feared by the slaves were those who came to buy slaves to be rowers

12

in Roman ships. This work was so hard, and the dangers of the sea and war at sea were so great, that rowers were lucky if they were still alive after two years.

It was a little better, though not much, to be sold to a Roman circus master to be trained as a gladiator for the show-fights put on for the entertainment of the Roman crowds. The gladiator at least had a weapon in his hand and could fight like a man. If he was lucky, and managed to survive his contests against other gladiators, or wild animals, he might even regain his freedom. It was the same for the slaves who were bought to drive chariots in the chariot races, another entertainment which drew large, excited crowds.

Gladiator fights and chariot races were usually after-dinner entertainments, although some shows were put on during the afternoon. Late in the afternoon, after four o'clock, the first of the carts, coaches, wagons and wine tankers allowed into Rome since sunrise would rumble into the city. As evening drew near, crowds flocked to the eating houses and the drinking inns to begin a night's rowdy merry-making. As darkness came over the city, oil lamps were lit inside the houses.

In the dark, unlit streets torch-bearers provided safety against thieves or attackers as they accompanied Romans to a friend's house for dinner.

The watchmen of Rome, the "vigiles", also came out in force. Their work in maintaining law and order in Rome was considered so important that they were formed along semi-military lines. There were seven thousand vigiles, one thousand in each of seven cohorts. They were commanded by a "praefectus vigilum" (prefect of police).

Every night was busy for the vigiles of ancient Rome, for they were the firemen as well as the night police for the city's fourteen districts. Fights, arguments, robberies, murders, drunken brawls, accidents — the vigiles had to deal with disorders and disturbances of all sorts. Fires could suddenly blaze up and consume entire "insulae" or tenement blocks in a matter of minutes. The vigiles had to be there to try to put out the fire, rescue people who were trapped, and keep back the curious crowds. The vigiles also had to make sure that the traffic kept moving. If a delivery cart or wagon got stuck in one of the narrow streets, it was they who had to remove it.

Far out in the countryside yet another flood of visitors would be slowly moving towards Rome. Behind them were thousands more who would come pouring into Rome at sunrise the next day or the day after. No wonder Rome, the heart of the Empire, was never quiet, calm or asleep for a single moment.

9 A Roman ship transporting wine. Slaves dreaded being bought to serve as rowers

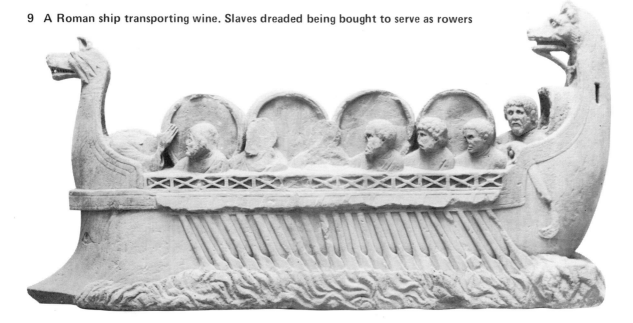

2 When Rome and its Traditions began

Every civilized (that is, settled and organized) nation in the world seems to have myths and legends about its earliest days. These most often tell of mighty heroes performing magnificent, sometimes magical deeds and enduring amazing hardships and dangers. In other words, nations often see the people from whom they are descended as supermen and women.

Actual history is very different and reveals a much more humble picture. The fact is that most nations begin with a few small settlements where the inhabitants farm the land and live a hard, simple life. Slowly a community grows up, increases in size and then spreads out to join up with its neighbours. So, the nucleus of a city is born.

The earliest Romans

Eight centuries or so before Rome became the centre of a rich, powerful empire, small farming communities were quite probably developing in this way on and around the Palatine, one of the seven hills where Rome later stood. Here in two villages the earliest Romans lived in oblong "capanne" huts made from wood and wicker-work, plastered with clay and thatched with straw. On the rich pasture-land surrounding the two villages the Romans planted their crops of grain and tended their flocks.

Like most small communities of this kind, the early Romans were always ready to defend their land, their lives and their freedom by fighting against marauding neighbours. In this context the Palatine hill was a good choice of place to live, for it was flat-topped and could be easily defended. In addition, it was the safest place in the area to cross the river Tiber.

This account of the beginning of Rome sounds very ordinary and, of course, it was. Later Romans preferred to think that their ancestors were more glamorous.

Romulus and Remus

The Romans believed that their city had been founded in 753 BC, not by ordinary farmers, but by Romulus and Remus, in mythology the twin sons of the war god Mars. The twins were descended, the Romans believed, from the Trojan Aeneas, a great hero of the war between Troy and Greece in the thirteenth century BC. Aeneas had founded Lavinium, about twelve miles to the north of the future Rome, and here, five centuries later, Romulus and Remus were thrown into the river Tiber by their jealous great-uncle, Amulius. But the two boys did not drown. They floated ashore near the future site of Rome. There, they were at first suckled by a she-wolf until a peasant found them and brought them up as his own children.

When they grew up, Romulus and Remus founded the city of Rome. Remus made fun of the wall which his brother was building, and for this insult, Romulus killed him. After completing the city, Romulus, according to Roman legend, became its first king. Here Roman history and Roman legend start to agree, for in its first two centuries Rome was certainly ruled by kings.

10   A wall painting of Aeneas, hero of the Trojan War. His son, Ascanius cries as Aeneas' wound is tended

...ding of Rome

...true, as archaeologists have recently ...d, that Rome was becoming a very fine city during this time. The most important improvement took place in about 575 BC, when the "Cloaca Maxima" (Great Sewer) was built to drain the marshland between the Palatine and Capitoline hills.

11 The forum was built on marshland which had been drained by means of the Cloaca Maxima. After the fall of the Roman Empire, many of the buildings were taken apart and the building materials used. The remains at the front of this photograph are of the Temple of Castor and Pollux

Rome thus gained a centre for its most important activities. On the land which had once been marsh, the Romans built a paved forum, with shops and colonnades and a great rectangular meeting place in the centre. Compared with Imperial Rome, which was to achieve such grandeur, early Rome was still a fairly modest place. However, the Romans had taken the first step away from the simple farming life to the organized life of the town.

Roman heroes and virtues

The influence of myth and legend remained and played an important part in the stories which later Roman children learned about

how the Romans threw out their kings and in 508 BC founded a republic.

The last king of Rome, Tarquinius Superbus, was a tyrant. What was more, his son disgraced a Roman lady, Lucretia, who killed herself in her shame and distress. If there was one thing the Romans detested, it was tyranny. If there was one thing they highly prized, it was personal honour. Therefore, they had to remove Tarquinius and his family.

According to legend, the war in which the Romans threw Tarquinius out and drove away his allies was won by tremendous heroes. One, Horatius, stood alone on the Sublican bridge which led into the city of Rome. There he kept the Etruscan allies of Tarquinius at bay while the Romans chopped down the bridge behind him. The bridge collapsed into the Tiber and the Etruscans had lost that way into the city. Horatius, wearing full armour, dived into the river and swam to the Roman shore.

When the Etruscans later laid siege to Rome, a young patrician (aristocrat) called Gaius Mucius slipped out of the city and made for the camp of the Etruscan king, Porsenna. Gaius intended to kill Porsenna but he was captured and threatened with torture and death unless he helped the Etruscans. The young Roman's reply was to thrust his hand into a fire and hold it there until it was burnt away. Gaius was afterwards given the name "Scaevola" which meant "left-handed".

Horatius, Gaius Mucius Scaevola and other heroes typified all that was most admired in the Roman character — loyalty to the community, determination, personal courage and self-sacrifice for the sake of the nation, discipline and success in war. Right up to the ending of the Roman Empire in about 476 AD these virtues were regarded as the best qualities in the Roman character. This was so even in the later days of the Empire, when Roman society became corrupt and luxury-loving, the army became

weak through internal quarrels and the Roman Emperors grew into wicked despots. Even then there was always someone to protest loudly and angrily that the traditional Roman virtues were being betrayed. Very often they were regarded as the traditional virtues of the Roman *republic*.

These special qualities enabled the Romans to conquer first the peninsula of Italy (by 275 BC), next the empire of their great rivals, the Carthaginians (by 149 BC), and finally, by the time of the first Roman Emperor, Augustus (27 BC-14 AD), an empire which stretched from the borders of Scotland in the north to the deserts of Arabia in the south.

Cruelty

It is, however, a fact of life and history that, as well as these virtues, Empire builders must have a touch of cruelty and ruthlessness. The early Romans, for instance, sought to preserve the health and strength of their community by killing off its weaker members. In the early days of ancient Rome a child's right to grow up depended on not being born sickly, malformed, mentally abnormal or handicapped in any way. Children born with handicaps like these were likely to be killed soon after they were born. They were either put to the sword or left on the mountain-side to starve to death or be killed and eaten by wild dogs and other savage animals.

To us, of course, this sounds appalling. Later Romans felt the same. However, the purpose of the early Romans was to survive, and to survive, what was more, in a harsh, primitive and dangerous world. Every Roman had to be strong and healthy, so that he could play his part in cultivating the fields and growing food, and take up arms to fight attacking enemies. Such people also had the best chance of having strong, healthy children of their own to carry on after them. If this were not so, then Roman society as a whole would be weakened.

Unwanted children

Sadly, in early Roman times it was also possible for perfectly healthy children to be killed off because they were born into families that were already too large. This applied particularly to girls, for girls were not generally big and strong and able to do hard work in the fields and fight in wars. King Romulus is supposed to have passed a law requiring the Romans to care for all their sons but only the first of their daughters. Not surprisingly, therefore, the early Romans seemed to consider that one daughter in a family was quite enough, and daughters

18

14 Reaping on a Roman farm

born afterwards were something of a disaster.

Of course, handicapped or "surplus" children were not automatically taken away from their parents and killed. The early Romans realized that there might be all sorts of other reasons why parents might pronounce one of their children unwanted. The parents might not be happy in their marriage. Perhaps they were very poor. Perhaps they were extremely shocked and disappointed at having yet another daughter or producing a child who was handicapped: in this frame of mind, they might decide too hastily to get rid of the child and regret it afterwards.

Therefore five of the parents' neighbours had to examine an "unwanted" child and agree with the parents that the infant should be killed. Until this was done, no action was taken. Besides, King Romulus had also decreed that no one had the right to kill a child who was less than three years old. By the time the child was three, parents could see if what had seemed like a handicap at birth had simply been a temporary condition. And the parents of a handicapped child, or a child they were too poor to support, would know with greater certainty whether or not they really wanted to end the child's life.

3 Following in a Roman Father's Footsteps

The father, not the mother, decided whether a child should live or die in the days of early Rome. The decision was not even the joint responsibility of both parents unless, of course, a man and his wife wished to decide such matters together. To the Romans, the dominance of the father was quite logical. Boys were more important than girls in a society like theirs, which required physical strength, stamina and fighting abilities. Therefore it followed that a father was more important than a mother when it came to big decisions.

The paterfamilias

A Roman father had absolute power over all his children for as long as he lived. This was so even when he was very old and his children had children of their own. A man or woman whose own father was still alive therefore had no rights over their own sons or daughters, no rights to own property, no rights to do anything on their own initiative. The father of the family — the "paterfamilias" — decided everything.

15 One of the Roman Emperors watching a fight between gladiators (see page 49).

The idea of the paterfamilias emerged very early in the history and traditions of Rome. And the tradition lasted throughout the twelve centuries between Rome's beginnings and the crumbling of the Roman Empire in Europe in about 476 AD.

When the Roman republic ended in about 30 BC, after years of civil war, Rome and the Romans needed a strong ruler. That ruler was Octavius, nephew of the famous Julius Caesar and the victor in the civil war. Octavius became the first of the Roman Emperors

16 Husband and wife, from a wall painting found at Pompeii (see page 38). These faces could almost be those of modern Italians

under the name of Augustus.

Why did the Romans, who never lost their fear and dislike of kings and never forgot the tyranny of the hated Tarquinius, still accept the rule of the much more powerful emperors? There is a clue to the answer in one of the names which Augustus accepted after 27 BC, when he became the supreme power in the Roman world. The name was "pater patriae", "father of his people". It is not very difficult to guess what sort of father Augustus proved to be to his people, for he had before him the model of the paterfamilias.

By the time he died in 14 AD Augustus had much the same power over the Roman Empire as the paterfamilias had over his family. Fortunately for the Romans, Augustus lived up to his name, which meant "worthy of trust and respect". For the family, as for the Empire, all was well if the paterfamilias was a father of this calibre. However, if the Emperor or paterfamilias was a tyrant, or cruel, or irresponsible, the lives of the people he ruled would be utterly miserable.

A paterfamilias, for instance, had the right to demand instant obedience from his children, no matter what task he required of them. If he wished to sell his son or daughter or other member of the family into slavery, he could do so. And there was nothing to prevent him from killing, or flogging or otherwise punishing members of his family for some misdemeanour, if he so decided.

This power of life and death in the hands of the paterfamilias was tragically demonstrated during the fight to throw out King Tarquinius in the sixth century BC. Two sons of Lucius Junius Brutus plotted to help Tarquinius regain his throne. Brutus, however, was one of the first two Roman consuls (magistrates) who were appointed to rule the city in place of the king. When he discovered what his sons had done, Brutus personally sentenced them to death. He considered that their betrayal of the Roman state was so

17 A boy slave asleep

terrible a crime that even the fact that they were his own flesh and blood did not stop him from ordering their execution.

23

When the paterfamilias died, his eldest son took his place and assumed all his powers. Younger brothers and, of course, sisters therefore lived their entire lives under the domination of the father of their family.

The immense power of the paterfamilias was not power without responsibility. Once he had decided which of his children he was going to bring up to take their place in the Roman world, he was bound by the Roman tradition to educate them:

ut omnes liberos susceptos educarent necesse est — it is necessary that all chosen to be raised (brought up) must be educated.

The paterfamilias therefore had all the responsibility for turning his children into good citizens of Rome and into men and women worthy of its traditions and its virtues.

Naming the children

A father's first duty was to see that his sons and daughters were properly named according to ancient tradition. The naming ceremony took place either at home or in a temple when a boy was nine days old and a girl eight days old. The child was consecrated, that is, dedicated to the Roman state and its gods, and a "bulla" was hung round his or her neck. The bulla was a lucky charm in the shape of a heart and it was meant to keep evil influences away from the child. The children of rich parents had bullas made of gold. The bullas worn by poorer children were made of leather. Boys wore their bullas until they left school, which was usually between the ages of fourteen and sixteen. Girls wore their bullas until they married.

The names given to Roman children at these ceremonies identified them not only as individuals, but as members of a particular family, and as descendants of a particular clan or tribe. For instance, a boy might have been named Marcus Cornelius Orbilio.

Marcus was his own name — his "praenomen". Cornelius was the name of his tribe — his "nomen". Orbilio was the name of his family — his "cognomen". The sister of Marcus Cornelius Orbilio would not have a praenomen, or name of her own. She would be called Cornelia Orbilionis. "Cornelia" was the feminine form of the clan name, Cornelius. "Orbilionis" (of Orbilio) was the possessive form of the family name. "Cornelia Orbilionis" therefore meant "a female of the tribe Cornelius, the daughter of Orbilio".

Educating the children

The paterfamilias had the power to decide whether the children went to school or were educated at home, how much education they should have, and who should be their teacher. There was no such thing as a system of state education in the world of ancient Rome.

Children did not normally start school until the age of seven. By that time, however, they had already had several years of education in the part they were expected to play in the life of the family. The first lesson was to know the importance of honouring Vesta, the Roman goddess of the hearth. The Romans looked on the hearth as the centre of family life. Here the fire burned which was used to cook food, and food was the stuff of life. The food itself was guarded by spirits known as "penates". Every Roman house also had its own "lar familiaris", that is, household deity. This god was worshipped at the "lararium" — the shrine of the lar familiaris. Romans often used to speak of fighting for the sake of "lares et penates". By this they meant fighting to protect and preserve what they considered to be the most important and precious things in life — we might say "hearth and home".

This idea was impressed on children from a very early age. As soon as they were old enough to understand, they were taken every morning to watch their parents pay reverence to the goddess of the hearth and make offerings of corn, flowers or wine to the lar familiaris. Whenever there was a special problem in the family or some tragedy or crisis, extra prayers were offered and petitions for help made at the lararium.

Children attended these occasions, of course, and when they were old enough, they used to offer their own prayers and petitions.

18 A lararium – an altar to the household god

Naturally, when doing so, they followed the strict instructions given them by their parents.

Boys

Sons were trained by their fathers for the roles they would have to play in life; daughters by their mothers. In the early days of Rome the boys had to toughen themselves up by running, jumping, swimming in fast-flowing rivers, and enduring extremes of heat and cold without complaint or weakness. They were shown how to throw spears, fight while wearing armour, ride horses and wrestle. For their tasks as farmers, they were taught to plough, sow, reap and tend animals. Later, when the Romans were no longer simple soldier-farmers, the cleverer boys learned law, politics and rhetoric, the art of making public speeches. They learned some of these subjects from schoolmasters, but their fathers were also important in training them to play their part in the public and political life of Rome.

Boys would sit close by when their father received visitors or clients who came to him for advice or decisions. In this way, a boy would learn the responsibilities undertaken

19 **Making a sacrifice to the Lares**

by a father who was a consul, or a landowner or a "praetor" (army commander). When fathers went to visit business friends, they took their sons with them. During dinner the boys would help serve the food and drink and listen to the talk of the adults. Again, when fathers went to speak in public, the boys listened, and learned by their example so that one day, when their turn came to do the same things, it would all be familiar to them.

If a boy was the son of a patrician (a Roman aristocrat), he could expect to spend a short time in the army as a "tribunus laticlavius" (chief tribune). Then when he was twenty-five he would become a member of the Roman Senate. The Senate was rather like the British parliament. It was the governing council of ancient Rome.

In a society as ordered and disciplined as Roman society, there was no doubt that sons would follow in their father's footsteps, and that girls would follow in their mother's.

Girls
Girls learned their tasks and duties in the home from their mothers. They were taught how to keep the household fire burning,

20 Tending sheep

fetch water, prepare and cook food, spin and weave cloth and generally ensure that the home ran smoothly.

In the days of the Roman Empire rich Roman families had armies of slaves to perform these mundane tasks. Rich women were able to laze around for most of the day if they wanted to. Or they spent their time calling on friends, painting themselves with cosmetics and doing anything other than housework. Some rich women and girls never knew what it was to pour wine into their own goblets or dress themselves or do their own hair. They had slaves to do all these things for them.

Nevertheless, housewifely skills were still greatly respected. For Romans the ideal woman was still hardworking, diligent, skilful and a dedicated housewife and home-maker.

21 A consul making a political speech in the Roman forum. Boys would go with their fathers when they went to speak in public, for when they grew up they would be following the same career

22 Girls may have been unwanted in very early Rome, but later on the Romans greatly respected the woman's role in life, and worshipped a mother goddess. In this carving of three mother goddesses the one on the left holds a swaddled baby, the next one has a clean swaddling band or a towel, and the one on the right has a bowl and a sponge

4 Plebeian Life in Ancient Rome

Only the rich or the patricians lived in houses in ancient Rome. Other people lived in well laid-out flats in three- or four-storey blocks of apartments called "insulae". ("Insulae" is the Latin word for "islands".) Insulae were built around a central courtyard and the better ones often had their own bath houses.

On the other hand, there were many squalid, rickety insulae where the poor Romans lived. These were badly built, unsafe, unhealthy and always over-crowded. Sometimes dozens of people lived in one flat. Two families, maybe more, might be crowded into a single room.

23 A model of some solidly built insulae. These do not look as if they might fall down. But many flats in ancient Rome were so rickety that they did collapse, killing all the inhabitants

Growing up in one of the over-crowded insulae was very different from growing up in a rich family in a clean, well-ordered, well-furnished "domus" (house). Even the slaves in a domus were better housed than the teeming thousands in the insulae. Patrician children could have rooms of their own, and slept in their own beds. There was a bathroom, and in the days of the Empire the domus was heated by hypocausts. This was a form of central heating. It consisted of a fire lit in the basement of the house which sent

24 A wealthy Roman home. There is little furniture; decoration is concentrated on the walls and floors (see Chapter 5)

warm air through the hollow walls and floor above. In winter, when Rome could be extremely cold, a domus heated by a hypocaust was a comfortable place to be.

A child of the Roman working class or "plebs" could never dream of such luxuries. At home in one of the city's insulae, there was no privacy. A room of one's own was out of the question, and a bed of one's own impossible. If the plebeian child slept in a bed at all, it was in company with three or four others and maybe more.

25 A water heater

Over-crowded insulae

There was a series of reasons why the insulae were crammed so full. First of all, because Rome was the great centre of the Empire and the most splendid city in the then known world, it was the place where people most wanted to live. Because there was so much demand for accommodation, prices in Rome were high, and so most people were unable to afford more than one or two rooms to live in. The landlords who owned the insulae realized that the more tenants they had to pay them rent, the more money they would make. Therefore they packed the people in without bothering about things like safety, hygiene or comfort.

Only those who lived on the ground floor of the block had running water or heating. Everyone else had to fetch their water from taps in the street outside or buy it from water carriers. There was one toilet on the ground floor, so most people living in insulae had to use the "forica" or public toilets. As they had to pay to use these, many tenants used slop-pails instead and usually emptied them out of the windows into the street below.

For building, the Romans since early times knew how to bind stones together with a concrete-like mixture of lime mortar, volcanic dust, sand and gravel. However, the poorer insulae were not always so solidly built. They were made of rubble and plaster inside a timber frame, or of cheap bricks which tended to crumble and crack. This made it dangerous for insulae to have too many storeys. The Emperor Augustus decreed that no insulae should be built to a height of more than 70 feet.

The dangers of living in insulae were extreme. It was far from uncommon for the whole block to fall down, killing many people inside and also anyone unfortunate enough to be in the street at the time. Many insulae in Rome burned down in a few minutes because a cooking stove had fallen over or a spark from an open charcoal brazier had set one of the rooms alight. Escape was often impossible, especially for people living on the top floor.

The Roman writer Juvenal (AD 60-130) wrote about the fearful risks of living in the insulae or even walking past them:

> There's death from every open window as you pass along at night . . . . Look at the height of that towering roof from which a pot cracks my head whenever some broken leaking vessel is pitched out of the window . . . you pray in terror that they will do no more than empty their slop-pails over you.

People living in these dreadful conditions were not surprisingly quarrelsome, violent, dirty and diseased. Children growing up in these surroundings quickly became what we call "brutalized", that is, coarse and cruel. Insulae were hardly the sort of places where children could learn the Roman virtues.

Future prospects for plebeian boys

Although life for a working-class boy was so different from life for an aristocratic boy, there was one thing in which the plebeian boy was exactly the same as the patrician. Like the patrician, the plebeian was usually destined to follow in his father's footsteps. The son of a road-clearer became a road-clearer, and the son of a porter, labourer, brick-maker, or water carrier had few other prospects in life than to do the work his father did.

If a plebeian child went to school at all, it was often for no more than seven years and usually for less than that. All he would learn was reading, writing and simple arithmetic. It was virtually unknown for plebeian parents to bother to have their children taught Greek and Latin literature or rhetoric or law which made up secondary education for rich or patrician boys. A knowledge of Greek was important for boys who became merchants, because Greek was the language of commerce. Rhetoric and law were necessary for boys who were going to enter public or political life.

26 Corn merchants

In the days of the Empire, however, such knowledge was of little use to plebeian boys. With Rome ruled by the all-powerful Emperors, plebeians no longer possessed the political influence which their predecessors had enjoyed at the time of the Roman Republic.

History of the plebeians

Only fourteen years after the Republic was founded, there was a fierce quarrel between plebeians and patricians. It arose because some patricians were taking advantage of the fact that constant wars and bad harvests had made many plebeians very poor. In order to survive, the plebeians had borrowed money from the patricians. When they were unable to pay the money back, the patricians made slaves of them. This was quite legal, because the Romans had the right to enslave anyone

27 A workshop. The plebeians who worked in such places were generally despised by the patricians

who did not pay his debts. However, legal or not, the plebeians were angered. As a result, in 494 BC they went on strike. They marched out of the city and set up their own state on a nearby hill.

The quarrel went on for a long time, but by the third century BC the plebeians had won a goodly share in the government of Rome. They could become consuls, marry into patrician families and even become "Dictators" in times of emergency.

By the time of the Roman Emperors, however, the plebeians no longer had such powers. Neither did the patricians in the Senate. The powers that had once belonged to the Senate had been greatly weakened since the days of the Roman Republic.

What did survive, though, was the disdain with which snobbish patricians regarded the plebeians. To them, plebeians were not much better than the slaves who did most of the hard, dirty, manual work in Imperial Rome. One of these rather high and mighty Romans was the great orator Marcus Tullius Cicero. In a book which he wrote for the guidance of his son Cicero advised:

Gentlemen should not soil themselves with means of livelihood which provoke ill will, such as collecting customs dues and money lending. Degrading and vulgar also are the gains of all hired workmen whom we pay for manual labour and not for their artistic skill, because their wages are the very badge of servitude. All mechanics are occupied in a degrading way, for no workshop can have anything about it worthy of a free man.

28 A poultry shop. Poulterers were among the tradesmen whom Cicero regarded with contempt

As for people who lived by certain trades, Cicero had great contempt for them:

Least respectable of all are the trades catering for sensual pleasures . . . fishmongers, butchers, cooks, poulterers . . . fishermen . . . perfumers, dancers and variety performers.

The work which Cicero described as "degrading" or "vulgar" was not only the most common work performed by plebeians; it was the work which kept life going in ancient Rome. No one knows, of course, if the plebeians were aware of or cared about the stigma which Cicero put upon them and their work. All they did know — and plebeian children could see

34

from a very early age what lay ahead of them when they grew up — was that everyday working life was hard and exhausting. They also knew that there was a great deal of unemployment in Rome. However unpleasant their jobs were and however poorly they were paid, it was better than having no job at all.

The position of the unemployed in Rome was not hopeless, but it was degrading. They had to survive on the charity given to them by the rich or on the free wheat and water supplied to them by the state.

Life in the Army

There was, however, one escape into a more meaningful life for plebeian boys in ancient Rome. If they knew someone connected with the Roman Army who could recommend them, they could join the army as legionaries. The Romans had always been very proud of their army, and with very

good reason. It was the most disciplined, best trained, best equipped and most successful army in Europe. The Army had conquered the Empire and was absolutely essential to its survival. Along the Empire's borders, on the rivers Rhine and Danube, Rome's soldiers were constantly on guard against marauding barbarians. Their task was to prevent the barbarians from entering Roman territory. It was only when the Army failed to do this, in the fifth century AD, that the Empire began to crumble.

Life on the borders of the Empire was tough. There was plenty of hard marching to be done and Roman soldiers had to carry all their equipment with them. This meant marching with weapons, food, cooking utensils, saws, sickles and other tools needed to construct camps for the night, or do various repairs. Food was not very palatable. It consisted mainly of vegetables and porridge, and drink was usually bitter wine. There was also a certain amount of brutality in army life, particularly from the centurions who were in charge of the cohorts, or groups

29 Roman legionaries sculptured on the Antonine Column, Rome

ies. Centurions carried vine canes,
~~~ary who fell foul of them could
~~~~ scars of the beating he received for
~~~e rest of his life.

All the same, despite the drawbacks and hardships, the life of a soldier probably looked much more desirable to many plebeian boys than the dirty work and dreadful living conditions they faced in the city of Rome.

For one thing, a legionary joining the Army had employment, if he survived, for the next twenty-five years. If he lived to retire, he was given either a grant of land or a sum of money. In the meantime, he was reasonably well paid, and if he took part in a great victory over an enemy he received a bonus. In addition, a new Emperor often paid sums of money to his soldiers when he came to the throne: this was usually to make sure that the soldiers remained loyal to him.

The Roman soldier was not only a fighter, but an engineer and a mechanic. Therefore a legionary was able to learn and use many skills. The soldiers built the superb Roman roads, the bridges, aqueducts, great fortresses and defences like Hadrian's Wall in Britain.

Soldiers also had to be tool-makers, smiths, carpenters, stonemasons, in fact jacks of all trades.

Life in the Roman Army also offered an ambitious plebeian advancement that was virtually impossible in civilian life. For example, he could become one of the 59 centurions who headed each Roman legion. Next, he might rise to the ranks of the "primi ordines", the most senior centurions in the legions. The great dream of every legionary and every centurion in the Roman Army was to achieve the rank of "primus pilus".

To become primus pilus, the most important single centurion in a legion, you had to be well educated and a good administrator. Obviously, the chance to attain this rank did not come the way of every ordinary Roman soldier. However, for those who did attain it, the prospects after their one year in the rank were very rosy indeed. A primus pilus could retire on his grant of land or pension at the end of the year, or he could go on to even higher ranks in the Army. One primus pilus, called Pompeius Asper, rose to be a praefectus castrorum, a camp prefect, and so became an officer of very high and much respected rank.

30 Bridge built by Roman soldiers at Rimini

5 A Life of Luxury in Ancient Rome

Most people have an image of ancient Rome created by "Roman" films made in Hollywood. They imagine huge banquets, with richly clad men and women lying on beautiful gilt couches. Everything on the tables is made of splendidly fashioned glass, or gold or other precious metals. All the dishes are piled high with rich food. Dozens of slaves stand by with jars of wine to fill and refill glasses and goblets. Braziers burning around the walls give off sweet-smelling scents of the herbs and perfumes sprinkled onto them.

The diners are entertained by exotic dancers, tumblers, snake charmers, jugglers, fire-eaters and other performers. The whole scene is one of the utmost magnificence, luxury and comfort.

Although only the very, very few and the very, very rich or prominent Romans could ever have afforded such banquets or such

31 A nineteenth-century picture of idle luxury in ancient Rome. A very small number of wealthy Romans really did live in such houses

32 A reconstruction of one of the houses excavated at Pompeii

grand houses to hold them in, this cinema image is by no means an inaccurate one. There is archaeological evidence to show how very comfortably the Romans could live.

Particularly splendid Roman houses have been excavated at Pompeii, which was buried in twelve feet of volcanic ash by the eruption of Vesuvius in 79 AD. In Pompeii, which lies fourteen miles southeast of Naples, archaeologists uncovered delicate mosaic floors, beautiful wall paintings and frieze decorations, bronze statuettes, fountains and gardens skilfully laid out in courtyards surrounded by colonnades of fine pillars. Several villas in Pompeii had their own private baths, where the water was warmed by hypocausts. In villas like this, rooms were scattered with silken cushions, statues of gods and goddesses, carved lamps and candelabra and beautifully figured tables.

When a rich Roman ate, he did so, exactly as shown in "Roman" films, reclining on a couch. This was supposed to be beneficial to the digestion, and considering how much could be eaten at a Roman banquet, it was a very necessary aid. Dinner might begin with shellfish, hardboiled eggs, olives or smoked fish, washed down with plenty of wine sweetened with honey. The meal then went on to include several meat courses, all heavily spiced with herbs or smothered in sauces, and ended with cakes, pastries, fruit and nuts.

Rich Roman homes were virtual storehouses of fine things: Rhenish glassware and crockery, multicoloured bowls from Alexandria, enamelled crockery from Belgium, bronze finger bowls, silver cutlery and all manner of other luxurious objects.

Strangely enough, however, even the rich did not have a great deal of furniture. Tables, lamps, couches and, in the bedrooms, a storage chest and a raised dais spread with a mattress were usually all the furniture which a Roman house possessed.

33 A tripod table

Rich Romans preferred, it seems, to concentrate their taste for luxurious surroundings on the walls and floors. Mosaic floor layers were among the most important and sought-after craftsmen in Rome for this reason. It required great patience and skill to form patterns or make pictures out of tiny cubes of multicoloured stone which were stuck into a ground of stucco. The wall-artists of ancient Rome were equally skilful. They painted straight onto the smooth plaster of the walls and produced great rolling landscapes or delicate designs showing birds, leaves, flowers or animals.

Wealthy children

The children of wealthy families who lived in such splendid surroundings naturally had plenty of toys to play with. Their parents could afford to fill their pottery money-boxes with plenty of bronze asses or sestertii, silver denarii, or if they were particularly lucky and their parents were particularly indulgent, a golden aureus or two.

These children might have slaves of their own to attend to their every need. A child's personal slave would sometimes carry his books when he went to school, act as a partner in wrestling matches, or play ball and board games with him. A rich Roman girl would use her slave to help her dress and do her hair, and if she was old enough to help her paint her face with cosmetics.

Fashion

Rich women, like their daughters, had very little to do in life except adorn themselves with jewels and paint. They wore pendants, necklaces, anklets, bracelets, armlets, and ear-rings — sometimes all at once. They painted their faces with ceruse (white lead), outlined their eyes and darkened their eyebrows with antimony, and reddened their cheeks and lips with ochre.

Doing your hair — or rather building a hairstyle — could take many hours. Hairstyles in ancient Rome consisted of great

39

34 Romans reclined on couches for meals

35 Mosaic floor

36 Delicate painting on the wall of a house in ►
Pompeii

37 Building a hairstyle like this of tight curls and plaits was a lengthy operation. Rich girls and women were assisted by their slaves

relief was that shaving in Roman times was hazardous and difficult. Barbers used sharpened bronze or iron knives which often cut and nicked the skin. The face could be very sore for quite some time afterwards, because apart from water, there was nothing to protect the skin.

Baths

A much more pleasant activity for a Roman boy was to accompany his father to the public baths. The public baths were not only the great washing places of Rome, but next to the forum, they were the great meeting places for the men. Here men met to discuss business, sign contracts, exchange news and generally enjoy the company of their friends.

Meanwhile, bathing attendants rubbed their bodies for them with a mixture of oil and sand to loosen the dirt and scraped the dirt off them with a curved metal spoon called a "strigil". Either that or the Romans talked and joked together while sweating in the hot room, or lying on couches being massaged and anointed with sweet-smelling oils.

The ruins of Roman amphitheatres and the remains of Roman roads are left all over the territory which the great Roman Empire once covered. So too remains of Roman public baths, at which so many enjoyable and luxurious hours were passed, are widely found. One of them (Aquae Sulis) at Bath in Somerset has a bathing pool 80 feet long, 40 feet wide and 6 feet deep. The hot water entered the pool through a lead conduit, part of which still exists today. Bathers dived into the water from a stone in which you can see the hollow worn by their feet. The temperature of the water was about 120° fahrenheit (49° centigrade) which is quite hot, and the three springs which fed the baths could produce 540,000 gallons of water a day. The baths at Aquae Sulis had a "calidarium" or warm room, under-floor heating and a 33-feet wide circular bath for women and children.

piles of curls, waves, plaits and ringlets. Often, artificial hair was used. Most of it was taken from German slave-girls.

Rich people, then as now, were the people who made and followed fashion. In ancient Rome this applied to the men as well as to the women. Roman boys, however, did not look forward to the time when they would have to shave. For a long time, it was the fashion for men to be clean-shaven and they were doubtless greatly relieved when, in the second century AD, it became more fashionable to wear a beard. The reason for their

42

By Roman standards, however, the baths at Aquae Sulis were relatively small. The public baths in Rome itself were sometimes enormous. A truly huge construction was the Baths of Caracalla, built by the Emperor Caracalla who reigned from 211 to 217 AD. The Baths of Caracalla were 1,000 feet square and could be used by up to 1,600 bathers at one time. Twice that number, however, were able to bathe in the baths constructed later by Emperor Diocletian, who reigned from 284 to 305 AD. Constructing huge and impressive public baths like these was one way in which the Emperors of Rome tried to make themselves popular with wealthier Romans.

The Emperors themselves were very keen bathers. In the third and fourth centuries AD, when Romans were becoming more fond of luxury than ever before, some of the Emperors used to take seven or eight baths

38 The Baths of Diocletian. (They are marked "Thermae Diocletianae" in the top left quarter of picture 2.)

every day. They also spent hours lying in "pensiles balnae". These were hammock-like baths slung from the ceiling by ropes. The pensiles balnae were the absolute peak of bathing luxury, for bathers were able to rock gently to and fro in the water. Naturally, wealthy Romans regarded the habits of their Emperors as fashions, and copied them. Many came to believe that bathing stimulated the appetite. And so really greedy Romans — and that often included the Emperors — used to attend huge banquets and then go straight from the dinner table to the baths. Their purpose was to get themselves into shape for another huge meal, but it was a dangerous practice. The result was all too often not a fresh appetite, but death.

43

6 Toys, Games and Entertainments

Toys and games

Beautiful toys for the children have always been a feature of life in well-to-do families. It was certainly so in ancient Rome. Roman children had miniature tea-sets, model soldiers complete with arms and armour, toy chariots with drivers and horses, toy animals on wheeled trolleys and all kinds of dolls.

Dolls were knitted or crocheted from wool, or made out of pottery, stone, metal or wood, with movable arms and legs attached to their bodies by metal pins. There were rag dolls and "Roman lady" dolls which could be dressed in changes of stolae (long tunics, as worn by women and girls), pallae (mantles or cloaks) and fibulae (fastenings like large safety-pins). When a Roman girl reached the age when she could be married, that is, around thirteen or fourteen, she had to put away her dolls and consecrate (give) them to Venus, the goddess of love, or Diana, the goddess of hunting.

39 Children with hoops and sticks

Roman children played with wooden hoops. They kept them rolling along by hitting them with a stick with spikes attached. Like children today, they played hide-&-seek and leapfrog, and they played marbles with small round nuts. There was also a game called "paganica", from the Latin word "paganus" meaning countryman. Paganica was played with a club and a ball stuffed with feathers and was rather like the modern game of golf. Paganica was not only a child's game. Roman soldiers seem to have been particularly fond of it, and some of them brought it to Britain when the Roman legions invaded in 43 AD.

"Harpastum" was a team game in which a hard ball was thrown from one player to another. It was rather like the modern game of rugby football. "Trigon", as the "tri" in its name suggests, was a game for three people. The players threw the ball with one hand and when it came round again caught it with the other hand. The one who dropped the ball the fewest times was the winner. In

another ball game, players used their hands to drive a ball back and forth against a wall. This was a favourite game to play after visiting the public baths. Baths often had a special court for the game attached to their premises.

These ball games were played by both children and adults. Both also played the game we today call blind-man's-buff. Both played with knucklebones, the predecessors of five-stones, and board games like backgammon and ludo.

40 Roman women playing knucklebones, an early version of "five-stones"

Public entertainment

In ancient Rome children as well as adults cheered and yelled to encourage their "champions" in bear-baiting or cock-fighting. Similarly, both adults and children went to the more cultural entertainments like poetry readings and music recitals played on lutes, cytheras and pan pipes.

The theatre

Like the Greeks, the Romans enjoyed going to see plays performed in the theatre. Roman theatres were semi-circular, with the straight side occupied by a long stage. It was covered over to protect the performers from the rain and to prevent the paint on the scenery from running. The audience sat on rows of stone benches in the half-circle part of the theatre, which was called the "orchestra".

41 The remains of a Roman theatre. The stage ran along the straight side of the semi-circle. Several theatres are marked in picture 2

The Romans copied much from the Greeks, the most cultured people of the time. Greek literature was thought to be the finest literature and many Roman boys whose parents wanted them to acquire the best education were sent to the Greek city of Athens to finish their studies. The Greeks also provided the Romans with the model for their theatres, and the plays of Greek dramatists like Euripides and Aeschylus were popular. Of course, though, the Romans had their own great dramatists too, such as Terence and Plautus.

Like the Greeks, Roman actors wore large masks while performing. These served partly as microphones to help project the wearer's voice all over the theatre, and partly to indicate the sort of role each actor was playing: a face with a tragic or sad expression for tragic parts, a smiling face for comic parts, or a woman's face for actors playing women's parts.

There were also performances of "cantica", a form of opera, which today we would call

"light entertainment". Roman light entertainment also included the "pantomimus", a masked dancer who performed in mime. Music for the pantomimus was provided by a chorus.

Chariot races

By far the most popular entertainments in Imperial Rome, the ones which drew the biggest crowds and attracted the wildest enthusiasm, were the chariot races and the gladiatorial combats. Roman Emperors were always very conscious that they had to keep the people happy to retain their loyalty. They did this by providing exciting distractions. As Juvenal put it in his *Satires*:

> *Duas tantum res anxius optat — panem et circenses* — he [the Emperor] limits the anxieties of the Romans to two things — bread and circuses.

▲
42 Masks like this were worn by Roman actors, to portray the character they were playing and to project their voices

43 Seventeenth-century engraving of the rectangular circus. Different sorts of gladiators are shown
▼

The "bread and circuses" method of keeping the Romans content was extremely successful. On public holidays there were free distributions of bread and huge colourful spectacles at the circus or in the amphitheatre. These spectacles had plenty of excitement and violence and danger about them. The roars of the big crowds at football matches today are nothing compared to the noise of the shouting, yelling and cheering of the crowds of up to 250,000 who watched the chariot races at the Circus Maximus in Imperial Rome. The Circus, which was not circular but rectangular, to contain the racing track, lay between the Palatine and Aventine hills and was 656 feet wide and 1,968 feet long.

Four teams — the Whites, Reds, Blues and Greens — competed in chariot races at the Circus which were conducted at very high speeds, even on the turns. A race consisted of seven laps round the circuit. Excitement among the spectators often mounted to frenzy as the horses' hooves thundered past, the dust rose in great clouds, and the drivers fought to gain favourable positions. The chariot drivers needed great skill and courage to control four or more horses, and accidents were frequent. Chariots collided with each other, or with the "island" that ran down the centre of the track, or they hit some obstacle in their path and overturned, throwing the driver under the speeding wheels of his competitors. Death or serious injury to drivers and horses was common. That, of course, was part of the excitement and thrill for the wildly enthusiastic spectators.

Gladiators

More scenes of feverish excitement took place in the arenas of amphitheatres where gladiators fought each other to the death or struggled with wild animals brought in from Africa and Asia. There were amphitheatres all over the Roman Empire, but the most famous — and the most blood-soaked — of all was the Colosseum in Rome. This huge circular building could hold 45,000 people.

When the Romans spoke of the "games", they meant the bloodthirsty spectacles that were staged in the amphitheatres. It is obvious what the games were like from the greeting which gladiators gave the Emperor or other important person who might be present: "I morituri te salute!" the gladiators shouted — "We, who are about to die, salute you!"

No one knows how many thousands of men and animals were slaughtered at the Colosseum for the entertainment of the crowds. However, it is known that on one occasion, five thousand ostriches, elephants, giraffes and other animals were killed there in a single day. On another occasion, ten thousand gladiators fought in a single afternoon.

The gladiators took their name from "gladius", a short Roman sword, and originally, they fought as part of funeral ceremonies. The dead man was thought to need an attendant to accompany him into the world of the dead and so two "gladiators" fought until one of them was killed and could go with him. The first known gladiator fight in Rome took place at a funeral in 264 BC when three pairs of men fought.

Later gladiatorial combats for the entertainment of the crowds were not, however, simply sword fights. Gladiators had many different weapons and means of fighting. Some wore helmets and carried shields and swords. Others were "retiarii" (net men) who tried to entangle their opponents. There were also the "andabatae" who, it is believed, fought blindfold on horseback; "dimachaeri", men armed with a sword in each hand; and men who fought from chariots. Some gladiators, the "hoplomachi", wore full suits of armour; others, the "laquerarii", carried only a lasso as a weapon.

Obviously, the life of a gladiator could be extremely short, which was why gladiators were usually slaves, prisoners of war or

44 The Colosseum

45 The spectators in this painting are turning their thumbs down to show that they want to see the defeated gladiator killed
▼

minals. If a gladiator fell injured during a fight, his life was in the hands of the crowd. The crowd used to yell "Habet!" (He has him) when the gladiator fell. If he lifted his forefinger to beg for mercy, the crowd might raise their thumbs and shout "Mitte!" (Let him go), to show that they wanted him spared. But, if the gladiator was unlucky, the crowd would hold their thumbs parallel with the ground or downwards and yell "Jugula!" (Cut his throat). In that case the gladiator was killed straight away.

Gladiators who survived for long enough could retire. They were then presented with a "rudis" or wooden sword. However, thousands of men — no one knows how many — met violent, terrible deaths in the arena. It is not surprising that gladiators sometimes showed fear or reluctance to fight and had to be driven into the arena with whips and red hot irons.

The Roman Emperors enjoyed gladiator fights just as much as their subjects and one Emperor, Commodus (AD 162-192), himself fought in the arena on occasions. Sometimes the Emperors staged gladiatorial combats as part of the Triumph they were given for some great victory in battle. In 107 AD, when the Emperor Trajan was given a Triumph to mark his conquests in Arabia, ten thousand gladiators fought in his honour.

Triumphs

A Triumph was a magnificent spectacle and a great entertainment for the crowds in Rome. It was particularly enjoyable because it gave colourful visible evidence of the military might of the Roman Army and its leaders. As the victorious general or Emperor

46 The four-horse chariot used in a Triumph brings the Emperor Marcus Aurelius into Rome

(the "triumphator") moved through the streets, where the buildings were brightly decked with garlands, the crowds packing the route clapped and cheered "Io triumphe!" Hail, conqueror). The consuls and senators of Rome headed the great procession, with trumpeters behind them, followed by the booty and arms which had been captured from the enemy. After them came animals for sacrifice, usually white oxen with gilded horns, and then a group of prisoners.

Next came the triumphator, riding in a four-horse chariot, clad in purple and gold robes, and carrying in his right hand a laurel branch. In his left hand the triumphator carried a sceptre of ivory topped with an eagle. In the chariot with the triumphator stood a slave, who held above his head the golden crown of Jupiter. The slave also had the task of whispering in the triumphator's ear reminders that he was only a man, and mortal. This was to stop him from becoming big-headed. It was, however, a waste of time and breath with the Roman Emperors, many of whom had themselves proclaimed gods.

It was, of course, a tremendous thrill for Roman children to witness a Triumph and to realize from the spectacle what a strong and mighty nation they belonged to. Children were also taken to watch gladiatorial contests in the arena and to witness the danger and death that so often accompanied chariot races. The Romans were not squeamish about such things, and did not worry about the effect it might have on their children.

7 Unhealthy Rome

The average Roman could expect to live for about forty years. This is up to eight years less than people living in poor countries today. The average life expectancy in poor countries like Ghana, Indonesia and India is about forty-six, forty-eight and forty-one years respectively. In the world's richer countries today, life can last for seventy years or more.

There were some Romans who lived for a very long time, even by today's "richer country" standards. The Emperor Augustus, for instance, was seventy-seven years old when he died. A famous Roman school-

47 A Roman mother giving birth to a baby is helped by a slave girl on the left and a midwife on the right

master, Lucius Orbilius Pupillus, lived to be one hundred. These life spans were, however, quite exceptional, even among the rich who lived in better conditions and had better chances of survival than others. Only about half the children of wealthy homes in ancient Rome lived to reach their twentieth birthdays, and even fewer in the homes of the poor.

This may seem surprising, since the Romans, even the poor ones, were relatively clean people with good public bathing and toilet facilities at their disposal. Even the small Roman towns in the Empire had their public baths, and like Rome, they were supplied with fresh water by means of aqueducts. In addition, the Greek doctors in ancient Rome were among the cleverest and most skilful of their time. Nevertheless, there was still a great deal of dirt, disease and lack of hygiene in ancient Rome, so that people living there were in danger in all sorts of ways.

Food was not always properly cleaned or prepared. Dishes, glasses, and eating utensils were not always properly washed after use. The water used could be polluted by flies and mosquitoes. In addition, not everyone used or was able to use the public baths. Among them was the vast population of slaves in ancient Rome. Soap as we know it did not exist at that time, and the hard soap made from tallow (the fat of goats) was too expensive for poor people to buy. A bar of soap could cost half a day's wages for a craftsman. Sewage and the contents of slop-pails were often emptied out of the windows of the poorer "insulae" into the street below — and this was a dangerous source of infection.

Diseases
There were epidemics of malaria, influenza, diphtheria, cholera and smallpox which killed hundreds of people at one time. One of the most feared and ancient of all diseases was leprosy. The Romans did attempt to stop the spread of this dreadful disease by isolating lepers (those suffering from it) in "leprosaria" or by sending them to some lonely and remote place where no healthy person was allowed to visit or come near them. Other diseases, however, raged unchecked and thousands died.

Even the childhood diseases which today can be prevented by inoculation were killers in ancient times. Roman children, like children for centuries after them, could die from measles, mumps, whooping cough or poliomyelitis (infantile paralysis). Many were born deformed or crippled.

There was, in addition, a good deal of child neglect among poorer Romans. It was not unknown for very poor people to cripple or blind their children so that they could send them out into the streets to beg money from passers-by. Many children died simply because they were not properly cared for. No one knew what vitamins or proteins were, and so children were often not given the sort of food which would enable them to grow up strong and healthy.

Infant mortality was extremely high. So many babies died in their first week of life that the Romans, like the Greeks, used to wait at least seven days before they chose a name for their children.

Doctors
The picture was not all dismal. The Greek doctors in ancient Rome were the finest of their time. They knew for instance how to treat sores or inflammations (swellings) with poultices. They used soothing ointments made from sulphur and other substances, and they also knew the health-giving value of fresh air, massage and proper diet and exercise. Rich people in ancient Rome often ate much more than was good for them, and after a particularly large feast it was not unusual for the Greek doctor to be called in to cure violent attacks of indigestion. The doctors gave their patients soothing liquids such as sodium or peppermint solutions to

MOGOVNVS INVOIIOIN

48 Sculptures of a doctor with patients

The Greeks also knew a great deal about surgery. They were able to set broken or dislocated bones, cut out abcesses, and could perform trepanning, that is, operations on the brain to remove pressure. The great drawback was that there were no anaesthetics to put patients to sleep. People undergoing surgical operations had to be strapped down so that they could not struggle with the dreadful pain they were enduring.

It was the same at the dentist's, and many people preferred to let all their teeth go black and fall out than to face the pain and suffering which going to the dentist involved. Fortunately for them, the dentists were able to provide false teeth.

It was even possible for people who had had limbs amputated to be given artificial ones. Everything depended, of course, on their surviving the intense shock and pain of having their legs cut off in the first place.

The attentions of the Greek doctors were expensive and only the richer Romans could afford them. Some were rich enough to buy their own doctors, in the form of Greek slaves with medical knowledge. Poor Romans, however, might never see a doctor in their lives, although they could get some treatment at an Army hospital. Hospitals and clinics for the treatment of the poor did not exist until the fourth or fifth century, the last centuries of the Roman Empire.

Charlatans and "folk remedies"

There were, of course, plenty of charlatans, the people who had no real medical knowledge, but offered weird "folk" cures for every kind of ailment. These charlatans were in a way the successors of the paterfamilias of early Rome who kept many strange powders, lotions and potions to cure his family of various illnesses. These "medicines" included the blood of gladiators, the dung and urine of animals, the brains of infants and the stomachs of seals. Charlatans used to administer such dreadful medicines while making mystical incantations and reciting

calm the pain, and warned them against the rich, oily, over-sweet food which had caused all the trouble.

"magic" verses. Although the whole treatment was really useless, it seems that the stranger the cure, the more sufferers believed in it.

The Roman writer Pliny the Elder (AD 23 - 79) commented:

> The physician is the only man who can kill anyone with sovereign impunity . . . to this, however, we pay no attention, so alluring [attractive] is the hope of a cure.

The charlatans of ancient Rome were often, in fact, more dangerous to life than the diseases of ancient Rome. There were probably thousands of men, women and children who would have survived their illnesses if it had not been for the charlatan's terrible "cures".

Not all "folk remedies" were like this, of course. Some Romans seemed to know of herbal medicines that cured more kindly, even if they did not know why they did so. Pliny the Elder, for instance, wrote in his *Natural History* of the curing properties of certain plants. According to Pliny, forty-two remedies could be made from lettuce, seventeen from parsley, eighty-four from rye and sixty-one from aniseed. Perhaps it was no accident that Pliny lived for fifty-six years, longer than most Romans of his time. Perhaps it was no accident, either, that the politician Cato (234-149 BC), who was devoted to eating cabbage, was eighty-five years old when he died. Cabbage is a rich source of vitamin C, which helps to prevent a frightful disease called scurvy and to keep at bay certain influenza viruses.

All the same, there was a great deal of

49 Lying in state

luck involved in living to a reasonable age in ancient Rome. In these circumstances, children soon became acquainted with death and its ceremonies. Children could be quite small — perhaps only four or five years old — when they saw their father or mother die and, quite probably, they had already lost several of their brothers and sisters.

Death

When a well-to-do Roman died, the body was clad in a toga. If the dead person was a man who had held important office, he was dressed in his official robes and a wreath of oak or laurel leaves — either the real, natural thing, or replicas made in gold — was placed around his head. The dead body was placed for some days in the "atrium" (hall) of the house, with the feet towards the door. The Romans believed that the dead were ferried across the mythical river Styx by Charon the ferryman. Therefore a coin was placed in the mouth of the dead person so that he or she could pay Charon for this service.

50 The ship on this tombstone was perhaps to symbolize the dead person's journey across the mythical river Styx

Then the dead body was taken through the streets on a litter carried by eight men. In memory of early Roman times when funerals took place only at night, torch-bearers accompanied it. In front of the litter musicians played flutes if the dead person had been young. Older people were accompanied to their graves by trumpeters.

An important part of a Roman funeral was the panegyric, which was recited when the procession had reached the forum: this was a speech made in praise of the dead person. The body was then cremated, or burned on a funeral pyre. (In Roman Britain, these pyres were made of pine branches.) When the fire had died down, the ashes were washed with wine or water, then buried in glass or pottery urns. In later Roman times bodies were not cremated, but were placed in stone or lead coffins and buried by the roadside. This was how the roads that led into Rome, such as the Via Appia (Appian Way) and the Via Ostiensis, were lined with the tombs and monuments of the dead. Only very famous or very rich Romans were buried in cemeteries inside the city.

As a preliminary to the nine-day mourning period, Roman funerals were followed by a feast. A sow was sacrificed to the earth goddess, Ceres, and there was a purification ceremony in which the bereaved family were sprinkled with water and stepped over fire.

Anniversaries of a death or the birthday of the dead person were commemorated in a similar way, and there were special periods during the year set aside for worship at the family graves. During the festival of Parentalia, which took place in the middle of February, the tombs of dead people were decked with wreaths, and offerings were made of violets, corn, wine, bread and salt. In May the graves were strewn with roses during the festival of Rosalia.

52 A funeral procession ▶

51 Part of a tomb found on the Via Labicana, three miles from Rome. The carvings represent the monuments and the temple on the Via Sacra, Rome

The poor went to their graves in far less splendour. Until societies were formed to help poorer Romans buy burial niches in one of the underground catacombs, a poor family might not even be able to hire four slaves to carry the funeral litter. It was more likely then that the corpse of a poor person would be thrown into a pit with dozens of other dead bodies at the public cemetery on the Esquiline Hill.

8 Travelling in the Roman Empire

The Romans were the greatest and most skilful roadbuilders of their time. They were also the first to build proper roads in the continent of Europe, and the last to do so until the sort of roads we know today were introduced late in the eighteenth century.

In the days of the Roman Empire, "all roads", as the saying goes, "led to Rome". It was not just a saying, of course. It was a fact. Twenty main roads began in Rome. Ten of them ran through the Italian peninsula, where they crossed the Appennines. And ten of them ran across the Alpine mountain range in the north of Italy, and then spread out into other roads which led to every

important place in the Empire. There were Roman roads leading into Spain, through Gaul (France), to Constantinople (now Istanbul), and through the deserts of Arabia and North Africa. The road system which the Romans built in Britain is more or less the base of our road system today.

Building the roads
The Romans built their roads as they built everything — solidly, systematically and with the intention that they should last. First they cleared the earth away and dug down until they struck rock or gravel. This formed the bed of the road. The bed was then filled

53

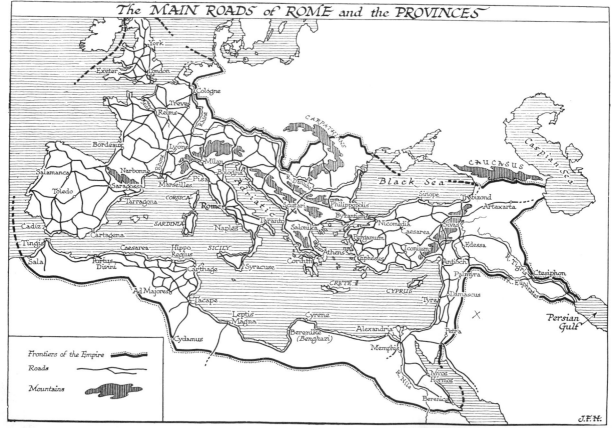

54 A modern road in Rome runs alongside the Roman road, with its five-sided paving stones

with rubble, stones, and flints. On top of that, the roadbuilders laid a layer of smaller stones and pebbles. This was then covered with a layer of gravel, that is, a mixture of sand and crushed stone. After this had been smoothed over, the roadbuilders laid thick pentagonal (five-sided) paving blocks of stone if the road ran along an important main route. These blocks, despite their great size, were cut so precisely that they interlocked. Finally they were packed with finely ground gravel to ensure a smooth uninterrupted road surface.

These magnificent roads were cambered, that is, their surface was curved, lower at the sides than at the top. Rainwater then drained off into the ditches at the sides. After the mid-fifth century AD when the

55 Horse-drawn carriage

Anglo-Saxons came to Britain and found the Roman roads, they called them "high ways" because of their cambered surfaces. The Anglo-Saxons soon discovered also that the Romans had built their roads in the best places to ensure good communications through the country. This was true, of course, thoughout the Roman Empire and was one factor which made travelling as fast as it could be while the horse still remained the main means of transport and haulage.

Safety of travel

People who used the roads within the borders of the Empire were assured of safety and security as well as speed of travel. The Roman Army, standing guard on the Rhine and the Danube, made sure of that. And there were also the officials who toured the roads to see that they were well kept and safe to use. Therefore, when the long summer holidays began at the beginning of July and the schools closed for about fifteen weeks, parents had no worries about sending or taking their children out of Rome to their villas in the country. Merchants transporting their goods along the roads were more free than they had ever been before from the fear

that thieves and cut-throats were lying in wait for them. This was an important assurance for the merchants to have, since they carried all manner of goods well worth stealing. These ranged from Egyptian corn, spices from Asia and Judean perfumes and cosmetics to glassware and pottery from the Rhine, oil from Spain, Gaul and North Africa and enamelled crockery from Belgium.

Speed — the straight roads

The Army too, who had built the roads, benefited from their excellent work when they needed to move columns of troops rapidly from one place to another. Similarly, the couriers of the Imperial postal service could carry letters and other mail swiftly from one destination to the next.

One of the reasons why travelling on the Roman roads was speedy was that most of them were straight. It was typical of Roman efficiency that their roadbuilders should follow the rule that "the shortest distance between two points is a straight line". But

56 The Via Appia, the first great road built by the Romans

it was not at all easy for the Romans to achieve their straight lines. They had no compasses, no maps, in fact, none of the equipment which civil engineers can use today and, in any case, they were building roads where none had been built before.

If they were building a road through hilly country, the Romans took their sights from one hilltop or high point to the next: in this way, they could decide the route along which the road could run straight. They were willing to make a road run round the bottom of a hill if they had to, but they also drove their roads straight through certain hills where the soil was not too rocky.

If the Romans were building a road through country covered in forest (as Britain and a great deal of Europe was in their time), they used to send a group of men ahead of the main roadbuilding party. These men would light fires as they advanced, and when the smoke from the fires rose above the trees, the roadbuilders knew the direction in which the road should go. This was how they built Watling Street, one of the Roman roads still in use in Britain today. Watling Street runs from London to Chester, where the Romans had a large "legionary" fortress, and there is a straight stretch of it which is nearly twenty miles long. The Romans used this "fire signal" method of routing a road in the desert too, where the land, or rather the sand, is flat, but totally featureless. Just as a traveller can easily get lost in the desert, because it all appears the same, so a road built in the desert can run all over the place — unless, of course, it was built by the Romans.

57 The Roman road-system extended throughout the Empire. This is the Roman "Marble Street" at Ephesus (Turkey)

Achievements in roadbuilding

By the time their Empire reached as far as the deserts of Arabia, in the second century AD, the Romans had been building roads for many centuries. Their first great road was the famous Via Appia (Appian Way), started in 321 BC. The Via Appia was called "queen of long-distance roads" by the Roman poet Publius Papinus Statius. To begin with it ran the 132 miles from Rome to ancient Capua (now Santa Maria Capua Vetere), but by about 122 BC, it covered the distance all the way down to Tarentum (Taranto), some 280 miles from Rome.

By 122 BC, of course, Roman power had spread through Italy and into the Mediterranean and the lands around it. Naturally, as the Empire spread, so did the Roman road system. By the second century AD the Empire was covered by more than 50,000 miles of first-class (stone-paved) roads, and 200,000 miles of secondary roads. One of the most extensive Roman road systems covered the entire southern shore of the Mediterranean, along the coast of North Africa.

58 Roman milestones. (See picture 1 of a carriage approaching a milestone.)

Along the roadside

Every ten miles, there were "mutationes" (changing places) where fresh horses, oxen or mules were kept. Wheelwrights were on duty at the mutationes in case a cart or chariot needed repairs. Every twenty-five miles the Romans built "mansiones" (stations), where officials could rest while travelling. There were also "tavernae" (taverns or inns) where other travellers stayed. In addition, there were posting stations for the Imperial couriers, where they changed horses or handed over their letters and mail to fresh couriers. By means of these relays, it was possible for an Emperor's letters to be carried fifty miles in twenty-four hours. There was also a private postal service run by Roman citizens, with slaves acting as couriers.

Roman roads were marked every thousand paces or one Roman mile (4,860 feet) with huge milestones in the shape of cylinders. These milestones weighed nearly two tons each. They showed how far they stood from the town where the road started and gave the name of the Emperor who was reigning in Rome at the time the building of the road began.

9 The End of the Roman Empire

Two attacks on Rome

In 390 BC a dreadful disaster befell the Romans. A horde of savage barbarian Gauls from north of the Alps invaded Italy and began to move southwards, towards Rome. A force of Roman soldiers tried to stop them at a stream of the river Tiber, but they failed. The Gauls swept on and burst into Rome, killing anyone who got in their way and destroying shops, houses and buildings.

When they left after three days of violence, robbery and destruction, Rome was a mess of ruins and hundreds of Romans were dead or had lost everything they possessed.

It was an appalling experience, but the Romans were a tough, proud people, who did not give way to despair. They rebuilt their city and made its protective walls stronger than before. They also reorganized their army into the most efficient fighting force the world had yet known.

Exactly eight hundred years later, in 410 AD, a horde of barbarians attacked Rome again. This time the invaders were Alaric and his Visigoths from across the river Danube. Once again, for three days the barbarians robbed and burned and destroyed and spread murder and terror through the streets of Rome. Once again, they left behind them smoking ruins and scores of dead.

This time, however, Rome and the Romans did not recover. The pride, energy and determination which had once made the Romans into conquerors and overlords no longer seemed to exist. Too many Romans seemed to prefer a soft life of luxury and leisure. Too many of the Roman Emperors had become weak, unpopular, and corrupt.

The decline of the Empire

Several Emperors had been murdered. One of them was Didius Julianus, who was killed by soldiers of the Danube legions in June 193 AD. Three months earlier Didius had gambled for the imperial throne and won it

59 Caracalla, Emperor of Rome, AD 211-217

63

60 A barbarian revolt against Rome

because his bet was higher than his rival's. The Emperor who succeeded Didius, Septimus Severus, turned the Empire into a military dictatorship, with soldiers holding all the important positions. Severus's son, Caracalla, conspired to kill his father, but succeeded him as Emperor in 211 AD. Six years later Caracalla (who built the colossal Baths in Rome) was himself murdered.

The Empire managed to survive for two centuries after Caracalla's death, but it was already rotten. As time went on, it grew more and more ripe for its eventual downfall.

All the signs of decay were there: bad rulers, political assassinations, the Army interfering in the government, discontent among the people and, by the time of Alaric and the Visigoths, attempts to appease rather than fight off those who threatened Rome. Appeasement, that is, trying to placate and please an enemy, has always been a sure sign of weakness in a government. Just before Alaric attacked Rome, for instance, the Senate tried to buy him off with gold.

64

The beginning of the attacks from the north

However, Alaric's Visigoths were only one among many barbarian tribes who, for many years, had been demanding that the Romans let them settle inside the territory of the Empire. Although the great days of the Empire were long past by the fourth and fifth centuries, it was still a highly desirable place to live. It was particularly attractive to the Huns, Vandals, Suebi and Allemanni who inhabited the untamed, uncivilized regions beyond the rivers Rhine and Danube.

Hoping to avoid a wholesale invasion, the Romans allowed the Visigoths into the Empire in 376 AD, on condition that they were unarmed and agreed to send their children as hostages for their good behaviour. The Visigoths, it seems, agreed, but the Roman generals did not keep their part of the bargain. Enraged by this betrayal, the Visigoths swept across the Danube and plundered, burned and slaughtered their way to Adrianople in Turkey. The Roman Army, once supreme and mighty, was unable to hold back the fierce invaders. This weakness eventually proved fatal to the continuance of Roman power.

The fall of the Empire

In 455 AD the Vandals led by Gaiseric attacked Rome and ran wild through the streets for a fortnight. They left half the city destroyed and littered with wreckage and dead bodies. The end was very near now, for the Suebi, Allemanni, and the Ostrogoths from the East flooded across the Roman frontiers in unstoppable hordes. In 476 AD a German called Odoacer seized power in Rome and made himself the first barbarian king of Italy.

At the time the Roman Emperor was a young boy. By one of the great ironies of history, he bore the name of Rome's first king and its first Emperor: Romulus Augustus. The young Emperor was a puppet in the hands of his father, Orestes, a patrician, who on 31 October 475 AD had driven out the previous Emperor and replaced him with his young son. For the next few months, Orestes ruled Italy in the name of Romulus Augustus. Then Orestes' soldiers mutinied against him and joined Odoacer, who had Orestes executed on 28 August 476 AD. Odoacer spared Romulus Augustus because he was a child, gave him a pension and sent him to live with his family in Campania in southern Italy.

There were no more Emperors in Rome after Romulus Augustus. The Empire had been divided into two parts in 293 AD, the Western Empire centred on Rome, and the Eastern or Byzantine Empire centred on Constantinople (now Istanbul). The Eastern Empire survived for another thousand years, until 1453, but the Empire in the West ceased to exist. With it went the life of comfort and wealth and luxury which the more fortunate Romans had enjoyed.

In the days after Odoacer came to power the Ostrogoths settled in Italy and part of what is now Yugoslavia, the Franks moved into Gaul, the Vandals ruled in North Africa, the Visigoths in Spain, and the Anglo-Saxons invaded Britain.

All over what had once been the Western Roman Empire, the splendid roads, aqueducts and bridges became neglected. The public baths, monuments, fora, fountains and beautifully laid-out houses and villas fell into ruins. People now began to live the rougher, more primitive, more agricultural life of the barbarian tribes.

For many centuries after the end of the Western Empire, children no longer went to school. They could not even read or write. Boys still followed in their fathers' footsteps and were instructed by them, just as Roman boys had once been. However, these fathers showed their sons a completely different sort of life. There were no more lessons in how to be a craftsman, how to build great temples, arches and monuments, or how to make speeches in public and take part in political life. Now, the most important things

for boys to know were how to plough fields, build huts, construct defences and fight against their enemies.

In the city of Rome itself, most of the ancient structures built by the Emperors were taken apart for building materials. Many splendid new churches and cathedrals were constructed, for Rome became the religious centre of Europe and remains so today for the world's Roman Catholics. However, after the end of the Empire, the population of Rome fell so greatly that a thousand years after Romulus Augustus only about 35,000 people were living there.

61 The sacking of a Roman villa by the Huns

Renaissance (rebirth). Not everyone agrees with these ideas. However, if you believe that the civilization of ancient Rome and its Empire were a splendid time, full of achievement, then the centuries following the end of that civilization were certainly "dark". In some ways, the darkness lasted a great deal longer than one thousand years. Nearly fourteen hundred years passed, for instance, before all children were once more given the chance to be educated and go to school. About the same time passed before the Romans' fondness for bathing once more became the concern of large numbers of people. Some thirteen hundred years went by before roads were built that were as well made as the Roman roads. It was almost thirteen and a half centuries before Europe began to know a long period of peace and security like the Pax Romana (Roman peace) which had existed under Roman rule. And some nineteen and a half centuries passed between the end of the Roman Republic in about 27 BC and the time when all the citizens of a country gained the right to have a say in the government that ruled them.

Not everyone, of course, admires the Romans or the Roman Empire. For at least two hundred years now the idea of having slaves, as the Romans did, has been regarded as cruel and savage. The bloodthirsty spectacles at the Colosseum and other amphitheatres are now considered disgustingly brutal. And conquering and ruling an Empire is no longer regarded as glorious.

All the same, the Romans gave much to Europe which later generations thought well worth copying or keeping. This is why, unlike most ancient civilizations, the Roman, like the Greek, has not faded away to become just dry, ancient history. In some of its languages, its road systems, some of its laws and many of its ideas, Europe today is what the Romans made it.

Conclusion

Historians have described the centuries following the end of the Roman Empire in the West as the "Dark Ages". Some believe that this period lasted for over one thousand years, until about 1550, when the culture of Ancient Greece and Rome was revived in the

67

Date List

BC 753   Traditional founding of Rome by Romulus and Remus

575   Forum built in city of Rome

509   Romans rebel against King Tarquinius

508   Roman Republic established

494   Revolt of the plebeians against patricians in Rome

390   Rome attacked and part-destroyed by the Gauls

275   Rome spreads its power throughout Italy

264   Start of the first war between Rome and Carthage

149   End of third Rome-Carthage war (Punic Wars)
Final defeat and destruction of Carthage

100   Birth of Julius Caesar

58—51   Caesar conquers Gaul

55/54   Caesar's expeditions to Britain

44   Caesar murdered in Rome

27   Octavius Caesar known as Imperator (Emperor) Caesar Augustus — First Roman Emperor

AD 9   Augustus fixes the frontier of the Roman Empire at the river Rhine

14   Death of Emperor Augustus

293   Empire divided into Western (Rome) and Eastern (Byzantine) Empires

313   Emperor Constantine adopts Christianity

410   Rome attacked by Alaric the Visigoth

426-29   Roman troops abandon Britain

455   Rome attacked by Gaiseric the Vandal

476   Last Roman Emperor deposed

1453   End of the Byzantine (Eastern) Roman Empire

Glossary

amphitheatre	circular theatre where gladiator fights were held
aqueduct	channel carrying water
basilica	Roman law courts
bulla	lucky charm worn round the neck
castrum	Roman (Latin) word for "camp"
centurion	commander of 100 legionaries
circus	rectangular theatre where chariot races were held
cognomen	name of Roman family
cohort	group of Roman soldiers (legionaries)
consul	one of two magistrates, elected each year to govern the Roman Republic, with the Senate
domus	Roman house
forum	central place in a Roman town
gladiator	fighter with a sword (gladius) who entertained audiences in the amphitheatre
insulae	blocks of flats in Rome
lararium	shrine of Roman household god
legionary	ordinary Roman soldier
nomen	name of Roman tribe
paterfamilias	"father" or "ruler" of the family
penates	household spirits and protectors
praenomen	personal name of Roman man
praetor	commander in the Roman Army
Senate	the Roman "parliament"
stilus	metal stick used for writing on wax tablets
strigil	spoon-shaped instrument for scraping off dirt at the Roman baths
toga	woollen garment draped around the body, leaving one arm bare
tribune	elected representative of the Roman plebeians
vigiles	military police force of Rome

Places to Visit

Roman Sites in Britain

Bath, Somerset — 1st century AD Roman baths.

Hadrian's Wall — Hadrian's Wall, which was built from the Solway to the river Tyne by Emperor Hadrian (AD 117-138), was intended to keep the Scots Caledonians from invading Roman Britain. The most interesting parts are Corbridge Roman station, Housesteads Fort and Chesters Roman Fort. The Wall was 73 miles (117 kms) long.

St Albans, Herts — museum containing model of the Roman town (Verulamium). There is also a hypocaust, remains of the town walls of Verulamium and a theatre.

Chester — site of Roman fort. Chester now contains Roman town wall fragments, mosaic pavements, and the "Roman Gardens".

London — exhibitions of Roman London at Guildhall Museum, British Museum, Mansion House (Temple of Mithras, excavated 1954).

Other remains of the Roman occupation of Britain can be found at Silchester, York, Wroxeter, Dover (Roman lighthouse), Lincoln, Colchester, Cirencester, Chichester, Leicester, Canterbury.

(Note: Names of towns ending in "cester" or "-chester" indicate that these were once Roman camps.)

Books for Further Reading

Burrell, R.E.C., *The Romans in Britain*, Wheaton, 1971

Cottrell, L., *Seeing Roman Britain*, Evans

Lewis, Brenda Ralph, *Ancient Rome*, How and Why Wonder Book, Transworld, 1974

Priestley, H., *Britain under the Romans*, Warne

Woolley, S.F. *The Romans*, University of London Press, 1972

Index

The numbers in **bold type** refer to the figure numbers of the illustrations